THE OFFICIAL
LIVERPOOL FC
ANNUAL 2021

L.F.C.

Designed by **Daniel May**

A Grange Publication

© 2020. Published by Grange Communications Ltd., Edinburgh, under licence from The Liverpool Football Club. Printed in the EU.

Photographs © Liverpool FC and AG Ltd., Getty Images & PA Images

ISBN: 978-1-913034-98-6

CONTENTS

Champions Of Everything	6
How The League Was Won	8
Premier League Champions Poster	14
We Are The Champions	16
2019/20 Facts & Figures	20
Jordan Henderson Profile	22
Wordsearch	24
Spot The Difference	25
Jürgen Klopp	26
The Kids Are Alright	28
Name That Tune	30
Kop Quiz	31
Top Of The World	32
My Liverpool	34
This Is Melwood	38
In A Town Where I Was Born	40
Sadio Mané Interview	42
Retro Champions	44
Colouring Time	46
Anfield's Three Graces	47
2019/20: A Season In Quotes	48
Anfield Crossword	50
Robbo & Milly's GOAT Lists	51
It's A Fact	52
Kop 10s	54
2020/21 Pen Pics	56
Winners Wall Poster	58
Quiz/Puzzle answers	61

LFC HONOURS BOARD

ENGLISH LEAGUE CHAMPIONS
1900/01, 1905/06, 1921/22, 1922/23, 1946/47, 1963/64, 1965/66, 1972/73, 1975/76, 1976/77, 1978/79, 1979/80, 1981/82, 1982/83, 1983/84, 1985/86, 1987/88, 1989/90, 2019/20

FA CUP WINNERS
1965, 1974, 1986, 1989, 1992, 2001, 2006

LEAGUE CUP WINNERS
1981, 1982, 1983, 1984, 1995, 2001, 2003, 2012

EUROPEAN CUP/ CHAMPIONS LEAGUE WINNERS
1977, 1978, 1981, 1984, 2005, 2019

UEFA CUP WINNERS
1973, 1976, 2001

FIFA CLUB WORLD CUP WINNERS
2019

UEFA SUPER CUP WINNERS
1977, 2001, 2005, 2019

SECOND DIVISION CHAMPIONS
1893/94, 1895/96, 1904/05, 1961/62

FA YOUTH CUP WINNERS
1995/96, 2005/06, 2006/07, 2018/19

FOOTBALL LEAGUE SUPER CUP WINNERS
1985/86

WOMEN'S SUPER LEAGUE CHAMPIONS
2013, 2014

CHARITY/COMMUNITY SHIELD WINNERS
1964*, 1965*, 1966, 1974, 1976, 1977*, 1979, 1980, 1982, 1986*, 1988, 1989, 1990*, 2001, 2006 (*shared)

RESERVE LEAGUE CHAMPIONS
1955/56, 1968/69, 1969/70, 1970/71, 1972/73, 1973/74, 1974/75, 1975/76, 1976/77, 1978/79, 1979/80, 1980/81, 1981/82, 1983/84, 1984/85, 1989/90, 1999/2000, 2007/08

Champions 2019/20!
HOW THE LEAGUE WAS WON

AUGUST

9th	**Liverpool 4 - 1** Norwich City	
17th	Southampton 1 - **2 Liverpool**	
24th	**Liverpool 3 - 1** Arsenal	
31st	Burnley 0 - **3 Liverpool**	

The opening month of the 2019/20 season saw Liverpool begin their march towards a first Premier League title in impressive style. The Reds got their campaign underway on a Friday night against newly promoted Norwich, to whom they showed no mercy;

League table		PL	GD	Pts
1	Liverpool	4	+9	12
2	Man City	4	+11	10
3	Leicester	4	+3	8
4	Crystal Palace	4	+1	7
5	Arsenal	4	0	7

racing into a four-goal lead by half-time as maximum points were comfortably secured. It laid down an ominous marker for what was to come, although a much stronger indicator of the potential within this team came in the victory over Arsenal. That was a result which left Liverpool as the only team with a one hundred per cent record and their four straight victories in August sent them soaring to the top of the table - a perch on which they would remain.

SEPTEMBER

14th	**Liverpool 3 - 1** Newcastle United	
22nd	Chelsea 1 - **2 Liverpool**	
28th	Sheffield United 0 - **1 Liverpool**	

Despite the added distraction of having to deal with games in the Champions League and Carabao Cup, Liverpool's focus remained firmly fixed on the prize that had eluded the club for so long. The momentum gained during the opening month was maintained through September

League table		PL	GD	Pts
1	Liverpool	7	+13	21
2	Man City	7	+20	16
3	Leicester	7	+8	14
4	Arsenal	7	+1	12
5	West Ham	7	+1	12

and as a result, they managed to stretch their lead at the top. When Chelsea were impressively beaten at Stamford Bridge, it sent out another statement of intent that Jürgen Klopp's team would be the side to beat this season. A touch of luck was required in the hard-fought win over Sheffield United at the end of the month but already there was a five-point gap between the Reds and the rest.

After 30 long years Liverpool Football Club are finally champions of England once again. The Reds are back where they belong and deservedly so. No one can deny that Jürgen Klopp's team were the outstanding performers of the 2019/20 Premier League season. This is the story of how a 19th league title was secured...

OCTOBER

5th	**Liverpool 2 - 1 Leicester**
20th	Manchester United 1 - **1 Liverpool**
27th	**Liverpool 2 - 1 Tottenham**

In what was Liverpool's most testing month of the campaign so far, they displayed remarkable resilience to preserve their unbeaten start. Deep into injury time at home to Leicester, the score was 1-1 when Milner kept his cool to score the winning penalty.

League table		PL	GD	Pts
1	**Liverpool**	10	+15	28
2	**Man City**	10	+23	22
3	**Leicester**	10	+17	20
4	**Chelsea**	10	+7	20
5	**Arsenal**	10	+1	16

At Old Trafford a couple of weeks later, Lallana came off the bench to rescue a vital point and deny United the prize scalp of becoming the first side to defeat the league leaders. Then, on the last weekend of October, not even the shock of conceding a first minute goal to Tottenham could knock the Reds out of their confident stride, as they recovered to claim a 2-1 win and preserve their six-point advantage.

NOVEMBER

2nd	Aston Villa 1 - **2 Liverpool**
10th	**Liverpool 3 - 1 Manchester City**
23rd	Crystal Palace 1 - **2 Liverpool**
30th	**Liverpool 2 - 1 Brighton & Hove Albion**

Saturday 2 November was a pivotal afternoon in the title race. With three minutes remaining at Villa Park, Liverpool trailed 1-0. It would have been a result that saw the Reds' lead at the top reduced to three points, but once again the never-say-

League table		PL	GD	Pts
1	**Liverpool**	14	+20	40
2	**Leicester**	14	+24	32
3	**Man City**	14	+23	29
4	**Chelsea**	14	+8	26
5	**Tottenham**	14	+3	20

die spirit of Klopp's team came to the fore. A dramatic late turnaround saw them snatch a crucial victory and when second-placed Manchester City were beaten at Anfield the following week, the gap between them and the reigning champions had widened to nine points. Two more victories at the expense of Crystal Palace and Brighton further strengthened the belief that this could finally be Liverpool's season. Leicester now headed the chasing pack but were still eight points adrift.

DECEMBER

4th	**Liverpool 5** - 2 Everton
7th	Bournemouth 0 - **3 Liverpool**
14th	**Liverpool 2** - 0 Watford
26th	Leicester City 0 - **4 Liverpool**
29th	**Liverpool 1** - 0 Wolves

December was a month that saw Liverpool competing on four fronts. The prospect of this hectic schedule taking its toll instilled a sense of belief in their rivals that ground could be made up in a Premier League title race that was threatening to turn

League table		PL	GD	Pts
1	**Liverpool**	19	+33	55
2	**Leicester**	20	+24	42
3	**Man City**	20	+31	41
4	**Chelsea**	20	+7	35
5	**Man Utd**	20	+9	31

into a procession. That belief was proven emphatically unfounded though as the Reds swept through the festive fixtures with a ruthless determination that saw them accumulate five straight victories, the highlights of which were a 5-2 demolition of neighbours Everton and a swashbuckling 4-0 Boxing Day success at Leicester. The team's lead at the top was extended to 13 points making it a merry Christmas indeed for Liverpudlians everywhere.

JANUARY

2nd	**Liverpool 2** - 0 Sheffield United
11th	Tottehnham 0 - **1 Liverpool**
19th	**Liverpool 2** - 0 Manchester United
23rd	Wolves 1 - **2 Liverpool**
29th	West Ham 0 - **2 Liverpool**

It was also a happy new year. In the league, 2020 began with another five wins out of five. It was a tough run of fixtures that Liverpool faced but every time a question was asked of them, they responded in a manner befitting their new moniker of champions-elect. When Mo

League table		PL	GD	Pts
1	**Liverpool**	24	+41	70
2	**Man City**	24	+38	51
3	**Leicester**	24	+28	48
4	**Chelsea**	24	+9	40
5	**Man Utd**	24	+7	34

Salah raced from his own half to seal a 2-0 victory over Manchester United, Anfield erupted and a realisation swept through the stands that there really was no stopping this side now. The Kop, previously reluctant to tempt fate, joyously shed its superstitious inhibitions to finally declare, loud and proud, that Liverpool were going to win the league and, if there was anyone out there who didn't know it already, they should now believe them. Come the end of the month, Liverpool had moved a cavernous 19 points clear of their nearest rivals.

FEBRUARY

1st	**Liverpool 4 - 0** Southampton	
15th	Norwich City **0 - 1 Liverpool**	
24th	**Liverpool 3 - 2** West Ham United	
29th	Watford **3 - 0** Liverpool	

Such was Liverpool's dominance of the league, it was now becoming a question of when, rather than if, a 19th title would be sealed. With new records being set almost every week, all other clubs had long since raised the

League table		PL	GD	Pts
1	**Liverpool**	28	+44	79
2	**Man City**	27	+39	57
3	**Leicester**	28	+26	50
4	**Chelsea**	28	+8	45
5	**Man Utd**	28	+12	42

white flag. There was no doubt that the trophy was heading to Anfield and pundits were left searching for new superlatives to describe the remarkable quality of this team. After Southampton were routinely beaten, there were a couple of scares as struggling Norwich and West Ham threatened to spring a surprise, then, out of nowhere, came the first defeat. An unusually out-of-sorts Liverpool succumbed 3-0 at Watford. Thankfully though, with the cushion of a 22-point lead at the top, it didn't really matter.

MARCH

7th	**Liverpool 2 - 1** Bournemouth	

This was the month when the new kings of English football were expected to be crowned. With the much-coveted prize now firmly in sight the shock of that first

League table		PL	GD	Pts
1	**Liverpool**	29	+45	82
2	**Man City**	28	+37	57
3	**Leicester**	29	+30	53
4	**Chelsea**	29	+12	48
5	**Man Utd**	29	+14	45

loss was quickly forgotten as the Reds got back to their winning ways at home against Bournemouth. It meant that if Manchester City – now a huge 25 points behind – failed to win their game in hand at home to Arsenal the title could have been secured when Liverpool made the short trip across Stanley Park for what was their next scheduled Premier League fixture. But then, everything stopped. The Covid-19 pandemic took a vice-like grip of the entire country. Football was understandably suspended as everyone went into lockdown and the inevitable coronation put on hold. Until when, nobody knew…

JUNE

21st   Everton 0 - 0 Liverpool
24th   Liverpool 4 - 0 Crystal Palace

After three months of lockdown, the return of football was eagerly anticipated, albeit behind closed doors and with extreme safety measures in place. For Liverpool supporters the champagne was on ice. Just six points

League table		PL	GD	Pts
1	**Liverpool**	31	+49	86
2	**Man City**	31	+44	63
3	**Leicester**	31	+30	55
4	**Chelsea**	31	+14	54
5	**Man Utd**	31	+17	49

were required to confirm what everyone had known for a long time. A goalless draw at Goodison in the first game back delayed the celebrations but a stunning 4-0 destruction of Crystal Palace at an eerily empty Anfield followed, putting the Reds within two points of their holy grail. They didn't have to wait much longer as the next night Manchester City lost at Chelsea, and Liverpool's lead at the top was now an unassailable one. For the first time since 1990 Liverpool could proudly call themselves the undisputed kings of England once again, and no team had achieved this feat in fewer games.

JULY

2nd	Manchester City 4 - **0 Liverpool**
5th	**Liverpool 2** - 0 Aston Villa
8th	Brighton & Hove Albion 1 - **3 Liverpool**
11th	**Liverpool 1** - 1 Burnley
15th	Arsenal 2 - 1 Liverpool
22nd	**Liverpool 5** - 3 Chelsea
26th	Newcastle 1 - **3 Liverpool**

League table		PL	GD	Pts
1	**Liverpool**	38	+52	99
2	**Man City**	38	+67	81
3	**Man Utd**	38	+30	66
4	**Chelsea**	38	+15	66
5	**Leicester**	38	+26	62

With the title secured the pressure was off but there was still the small matter of squeezing the final seven league matches into the space of just over three weeks. Liverpool suffered two more defeats during this sequence and surrendered their one hundred per cent home record, but opponents lined up to form a guard of honour for the champions at each of the remaining fixtures and the season ended on a high. A thrilling victory over Chelsea at Anfield preceded the long awaited presentation of the Premier League trophy, before victory on the last day at Newcastle took them to the 99-point mark, setting a new club record. It had been an unforgettable season in more ways than one.

The players show their support for the 'Black Lives Matter' movement by 'taking the knee' prior to kick-off.

15

WE ARE THE

How the manager and players reacted to confirmation that Liverpool were the 2019/20 Premier League champions…

"I AM COMPLETELY OVERWHELMED; I DON'T KNOW, IT'S A MIX OF EVERYTHING – I AM RELIEVED, I AM HAPPY, I AM PROUD.

I couldn't be more proud of the boys. I couldn't have dreamed of something like that and I never did before last year, honestly. We were not close enough three years ago, a year ago we were really close… what the boys have done in the last two-and-a-half years, the consistency they show is absolutely incredible and second to none. Honestly, I have no idea how we do that all the time. It is a wonderful moment."

Jürgen **Klopp**

"I COULD NEVER IN WORDS DESCRIBE THE FEELING OF WINNING THE PREMIER LEAGUE, JUST LIKE I COULDN'T DESCRIBE WINNING THE CHAMPIONS LEAGUE.

It's a unique feeling and one that, again, I'm very proud of. I've been so honoured to be part of this football club right from the first moment that I came and to go on the journey, to be with this manager, this group of players, these fans – it's been so special."

Jordan **Henderson**

CHAMPIONS

"I FEEL GREAT. WINNING AND BEING [A] CHAMPION IS ALWAYS SOMETHING SPECIAL, BUT BEING PREMIER LEAGUE CHAMPION FOR THE FIRST TIME IN THE HISTORY OF THIS CLUB MEANS A LOT FOR US.

I believe we put our names in the history of this club. We are part of something big here, we are doing our job on the highest level we can and we are winning great things. This is becoming something really special for me, for my life. This club will be part of my life and part of my history until the last day."

Alisson **Becker**

"IT'S SUCH A GOOD FEELING. EMOTIONAL BUT JUST FULL OF JOY.

We've worked so hard already this season. It's been a dream come true for all of us already. For me personally, coming to the club, winning the Champions League, winning the Premier League in the two-and-a-half seasons I've been at the club, it is just magnificent and a dream come true. It's something I always hoped for when I joined Liverpool. It's just amazing and it's amazing to be part of this group. It's amazing also to be with these kind of players, the manager, the staff, Melwood, all the people there looking after us. Everyone has to feel like a champion who is part of us, including the fans of course."

Virgil van Dijk

"WE PROBABLY THOUGHT AS A TEAM WE WOULD BE ABLE TO DO IT OURSELVES, BUT WE DON'T REALLY CARE HOW WE DID IT AT THE END OF THE DAY.

We are Premier League champions and we are proud of that. Obviously things are not as we imagined probably a few months ago or even a year ago how we imagined to win the Premier League, but we are not going to complain and make a fuss. It's something we've always dreamed of. As fans I think it's something that will always be remembered."

Trent **Alexander-Arnold**

"IT'S DIFFICULT TO DESCRIBE BUT I CAN SAY THAT I'M REALLY HAPPY AND REALLY PLEASED THAT I CAN BE A PART OF THIS TEAM, BE A PART OF THIS CLUB.

And I'm really happy that this time we can give this title to the supporters because they have waited so long for this title. The supporters were so loyal during the years since I'm here and even before I came here. That makes it more beautiful because when you have such loyal supporters and you can give them one of the best gifts, it makes it more beautiful than it is."

Gini **Wijnaldum**

"IT'S A SPECIAL MOMENT AND A UNIQUE MOMENT.

It has been a long [time] waiting for the title and finally we got it and you can see how happy the players, the staff, the manager, [the people] around the club, all over the world the supporters are. I always say that dreams are allowed and for sure last year we went really, really close: one point, but at the same time I can say congratulations for City because they for sure deserved it and won it and that's part of football. We showed this year great character and from the beginning we have been really, really consistent, which is really important for the team who has a dream and the team who wants to win something. For sure we showed it from the beginning until the end and the gap was so big for us. It's just an incredible moment for us."

Sadio **Mané**

"TO WIN THE PREMIER LEAGUE AFTER LONG YEARS FOR THE CLUB AND THE CITY, IT'S UNBELIEVABLE.

I can't describe with words, it's so hard to say [how it feels]. When I came here, I said I wanted to win the Premier League - it's my first thing in my head, I want to win the Premier League and the Champions League. People said, 'If you could choose one…?' But now I can say that I'd choose both! The Premier League, I can say now after we won it, for the city it is something else. Everybody is crazy about the result, everybody is crazy about the Premier League."

Mo **Salah**

STAT-ATTACK

APPEARANCES

Name	League	FA Cup	League Cup	Europe	Other	Total
Roberto Firmino	38	2	0	9	3	52
Virgil van Dijk	38	1	0	9	2	50
Trent Alexander-Arnold	38	0	0	8	3	49
Andy Robertson	36	1	0	9	3	49
Mohamed Salah	34	2	0	9	3	48
Sadio Mané	35	1	0	9	2	47
Georginio Wijnaldum	37	0	0	9	1	47
Alex Oxlade-Chamberlain	30	2	2	6	3	43
Joe Gomez	28	2	2	8	3	43
Divock Origi	28	3	1	7	3	42
Jordan Henderson	30	0	0	7	3	40
Fabinho Tavarez	28	2	0	8	1	39
Alisson Becker	29	0	0	5	3	37
James Milner	22	2	2	9	2	37
Naby Keïta	18	0	2	4	3	27
Adam Lallana	15	2	2	0	3	22
Adrián San Miguel	11	3	0	4	0	18
Dejan Lovren	10	1	1	3	0	15
Takumi Minamino	10	3	0	1	0	14
Joël Matip	9	1	0	2	1	13
Curtis Jones	6	4	2	0	0	12
Xherdan Shaqiri	7	0	0	1	3	11
Neco Williams	6	4	1	0	0	11
Harvey Elliott	2	3	3	0	0	8
Pedro Chirivella	0	3	3	0	0	6
Caoimhín Kelleher	0	1	3	0	0	4
Sepp van den Berg	0	1	3	0	0	4
Ki-Jana Hoever	0	1	2	0	0	3
Rhian Brewster	0	1	2	0	0	3
Herbie Kane	0	0	2	0	0	2
Yasser Larouci	0	2	0	0	0	2
Leighton Clarkson	0	1	1	0	0	2
Morgan Boyes	0	1	1	0	0	2
Tony Gallacher	0	0	1	0	0	1
Elijah Dixon-Bonner	0	1	0	0	0	1
Jack Bearne	0	0	1	0	0	1
James Norris	0	0	1	0	0	1
Thomas Hill	0	0	1	0	0	1
Nathaniel Phillips	0	1	0	0	0	1
Liam Millar	0	1	0	0	0	1
Joe Hardy	0	1	0	0	0	1
Jake Cain	0	1	0	0	0	1
Adam Lewis	0	1	0	0	0	1
Luis Longstaff	0	0	1	0	0	1
Isaac Christie-Davies	0	0	1	0	0	1

GOALS

Name	League	FA Cup	League Cup	Europe	Other	Total
Mohamed Salah	19	0	0	4	0	23
Sadio Mané	18	0	0	4	0	22
Roberto Firmino	9	0	0	1	2	12
Alex Oxlade-Chamberlain	4	0	1	3	0	8
Divock Origi	4	0	2	0	0	6
Georginio Wijnaldum	4	0	0	2	0	6
Own goals	2	2	1	0	0	5
Virgil van Dijk	5	0	0	0	0	5
Trent Alexander-Arnold	4	0	0	0	0	4
Naby Keïta	2	0	0	1	1	4
Jordan Henderson	4	0	0	0	0	4
James Milner	2	0	2	0	0	4
Andy Robertson	2	0	0	1	0	3
Curtis Jones	1	2	0	0	0	3
Joël Matip	1	0	0	0	1	2
Fabinho Tavarez	2	0	0	0	0	2
Dejan Lovren	0	0	0	1	0	1
Ki-Jana Hoever	0	0	1	0	0	1
Adam Lallana	1	0	0	0	0	1
Xherdan Shaqiri	1	0	0	0	0	1

TOP 3 PLAYERS WITH MOST ASSISTS

Name	League	FA Cup	League Cup	Europe	Other	Total
Trent Alexander-Arnold	13	0	0	1	1	15
Roberto Firmino	8	0	0	5	0	13
Mohamed Salah	10	0	0	2	1	13

CLEAN SHEETS

Name	League	FA Cup	League Cup	Europe	Other	Total
Alisson Becker	13	0	0	1	1	15
Adrián San Miguel	2	1	0	0	0	3
Caoimhín Kelleher	0	1	1	0	0	2

TEAM STATS

Total games:	57	Average attendance at home - league:	42,054
Games won:	41	Average attendance at home - overall:	44,844
Games drawn:	8	Average goals per game - League:	2.74
Games lost:	8	Average goals per game - Overall:	2.62
Clean sheets - league:	15	Average goal minute - League:	48
Clean sheets - overall:	20	Average goal minute - Overall:	50
Total goals:	117		

INDIVIDUAL AWARDS

FWA PLAYER OF THE YEAR

Jordan Henderson

LMA MANAGER OF THE YEAR

Jürgen Klopp

PFA FANS' PLAYER OF THE SEASON

Sadio Mané

LFC STANDARD CHARTERED PLAYER OF THE MONTH

August – Mohamed Salah
September – Roberto Firmino
October – Alex Oxlade-Chamberlain
November – Sadio Mané
December – Trent Alexander-Arnold
January – Mohamed Salah
February – Trent Alexander-Arnold

PREMIER LEAGUE PLAYER OF THE MONTH

November – Sadio Mané
December – Trent Alexander-Arnold

LFC STANDARD CHARTERED MEN'S PLAYER OF THE SEASON

Jordan Henderson

PREMIER LEAGUE YOUNG PLAYER OF THE SEASON

Trent Alexander-Arnold

PREMIER LEAGUE MANAGER OF THE MONTH

August, September, November, December & January – Jürgen Klopp

PREMIER LEAGUE MANAGER OF THE SEASON

Jürgen Klopp

HERE'S TO YOU...
JORDAN HENDERSON

We chart the remarkable rise of our captain and longest-serving player; a man who is fast becoming a serial trophy lifter and who, in 2020, was deservedly recognised by the football writers of England as the country's outstanding footballer...

- **June 1990** – a month after Liverpool lift their 18th league title Jordan Henderson is born in Sunderland

- **November 2008** – a decade after joining the youth ranks of his hometown club, Henderson makes his senior Sunderland debut

- **January 2009** – he is sent on loan to Coventry, for whom he makes 13 appearances and scores one goal

- **November 2010** – after impressing for England under-21s, Henderson wins his first full cap, lining up alongside Steven Gerrard in a friendly against France

- **June 2011** – after scoring five goals in 79 appearances for the Black Cats, Henderson is signed for Liverpool by Kenny Dalglish

- **August 2011** – he makes his Liverpool debut on the opening day of the season in a 1-1 draw against his former side, while later in the month he scores his first goal for the club in a 3-1 win over Bolton

- **February 2012** – Henderson is part of the Liverpool team that beat Cardiff on penalties to win the League Cup at Wembley

- **May 2012** – he returns to Wembley but is on the losing side as Liverpool are beaten 2-1 by Chelsea in the FA Cup final

- **June 2012** – after receiving a late call-up to Roy Hodgson's England squad, he makes two substitute appearances at the European Championships in Ukraine

- **April 2014** – Henderson is an ever-present in the Liverpool side that looks on course to win the Premier League, but he's sent off in a crucial game against Manchester City and misses three of the final four games as the Reds agonisingly surrender top spot

- **June 2014** – Liverpool's number 14 makes two appearances for England at the World Cup in Brazil

- **August 2014** – Brendan Rodgers announces that Henderson will take over from the departing Daniel Agger as vice-captain at Anfield

- **November 2014** – in the absence of Steven Gerrard, he captains Liverpool for the first time in a 1-0 home win against Stoke

- **July 2015** – Henderson is appointed Gerrard's successor as permanent Liverpool captain

- **February 2016** – Henderson leads Liverpool out at Wembley for the League Cup final but the Reds suffer disappointment in a penalty shoot-out defeat against Manchester City

- **May 2016** – despite battling back to fitness following a knee injury sustained the previous

364
Appearances

29
Goals

Honours:

- Premier League
- Champions League
- FIFA Club World Cup
- UEFA Super Cup
- FWA Footballer of the Year

month, Henderson has to settle for a place on the bench as Liverpool lose to Sevilla in the Europa League final

June 2016 – he represents his country at another international tournament, but features only once as England are eliminated at the first knockout stage of the Euros in France

May 2018 – a thrilling run up to the Champions League final ends in heartache following a 3-1 defeat to Real Madrid in Kiev

June 2018 – the Reds' skipper makes five appearances as England reach the last four of the World Cup in Russia

June 2019 – Henderson finally lifts his first trophy as Liverpool captain as he leads the Reds to a

Champions League final victory over Tottenham in Madrid

August 2019 – the 2019/20 season begins with Henderson lifting more silverware as Liverpool beat Chelsea on penalties in Istanbul to clinch the UEFA Super Cup

December 2019 – to cap a remarkable six months he then skippers the Reds to glory in the FIFA Club World Cup to seal an unprecedented international treble

July 2020 – Henderson becomes the first Liverpool captain to lift the Premier League title and is named FWA Player of the Year.

"To understand the story of Jordan Henderson, you cannot underestimate and should not forget that he had the most difficult job in world football – becoming captain after Steven Gerrard... Because it's not about who you are, it's about who the other one was ... How he dealt with that from the first day I met him, he was exceptional. How he grew in that role and, of course, how the way we play football helped him to be himself on the pitch. That all came together and I couldn't respect Hendo more... he's in the middle of his career and still greedy and desperate to win more stuff. But in 10 years when he looks back, he will be very, very proud of what he has done here."

Jürgen Klopp

WORDSEARCH

During the course of an unforgettable and triumphant 2019/20 Premier League season, Liverpool defeated every opposition team at least once. See if you can find all the beaten sides by searching the grid vertically, horizontally or diagonally…

```
W M D E T I N U D L E I F F E H S K B
X Y K W T M P Z F M M H C K Q H M R F
L K T N L R P G R A P C V G M T E Y D
F L N I C R V N L F T I N N R U V M E
B K N G C J J L Y M K W G X B O E D T
B U M G N R I B A Q T R L P L M R N I
V M R T R V E H R N N O T K T E T E N
L H J N N E T T V I M N L M N N O W U
Q K K O L S T T S H G N V Y H R N C R
H L T N E E V S F E O H K P K U M A E
L S Q W N K Y T E T H C T W L O M S T
A P N K T M M P C H C A O V B A T S S
A R S E N A L M W E I T N H N L H L E
J K N Y C R A B L B F E K A R T N E H
J T K G R H M S N O M T L R M F E C C
K W C T T L E Z R P G K N L C N T F N
K X K U V A T D S E V L O W M J T B A
M H O M B W V L Q F F R G N N N O B M
M S C R Y S T A L P A L A C E G T N Q
```

- [ ] Norwich
- [ ] Southampton
- [ ] Arsenal
- [ ] Burnley
- [ ] Newcastle
- [ ] Chelsea
- [ ] Sheffield United
- [ ] Leicester
- [ ] Tottenham
- [ ] Aston Villa
- [ ] Manchester City
- [ ] Crystal Palace
- [ ] Brighton
- [ ] Everton
- [ ] Bournemouth
- [ ] Watford
- [ ] Wolves
- [ ] Manchester United
- [ ] West Ham

SPOT THE DIFFENCE

See if you can spot the seven differences!

ORIGINAL

DIFFERENCES

ANSWERS ARE ON PAGE 61

25

THE BOSS

Jürgen Klopp

"I always thought about working in England because of the kind of football, the intensity of football. Liverpool was first choice. When I got the call, it felt right from the first second. Liverpool, it's a special place. You feel it when you make your first step. It's just great to do it for these people because you know how much it means to them. These people deserve it so much. Success in football lifts the mood of the city always and I hope we can use that for the better for all parts which are necessary for this city. I think one of the most important things I said was we have to write our own story and create our own history. That's what these boys have done now. They were legends before that in my mind, but now they are real legends and that's nice."

THE KIDS

Aside from the obvious disappointments of earlier than hoped for exits in the domestic cup competitions, there was plenty of positives to take from Liverpool's Carabao and FA Cup campaigns in 2019/20 – notably the outstanding performances of the club's youngsters.

While the primary focus throughout the season centred on the team's pursuit of its first League title in 30 years, it was no surprise to see Jürgen Klopp rotate his squad when it came to cup-ties and the Anfield starlets certainly seized their opportunity to shine.

Starting with the visit to MK Dons in the Carabao Cup third round, five debutants – Caoimhín Kelleher, Herbie Kane, Harvey Elliott, Sepp van den Berg and Rhian Brewster – took to the field. At just 16 years, 5 months and 21 days old, Elliott became the youngest player ever to start a senior competitive fixture for the Reds, while Ki-Jana Hoever, just one year older and making only his second appearance, netted in a 2-0 win.

Against Arsenal in round four, it was the turn of Neco Williams to impress on his senior bow, in a remarkable 5-5 draw that climaxed with Brewster and Curtis Jones among the scorers in the subsequent penalty shoot-out victory.

While Klopp and the senior squad were away in Qatar for the Club World Cup, under-23 coach Neil Critchley took charge of team affairs for the quarter-final away to Aston Villa and on a freezing night in the Midlands, a host of records were broken in terms of team selection.

The team selected to start (see p29) was the youngest and least experienced in Liverpool history.

CURTIS JONES

BECAME OUR YOUNGEST EVER CAPTAIN!

19	0	5
YEARS	MONTHS	DAYS

HARVEY ELLIOTT

BECAME OUR YOUNGEST EVER FULL DEBUTANT!

16	5	21
YEARS	MONTHS	DAYS

By the end of the match eight more players had made their debuts, with James Norris – aged 16 years, 8 months and 13 days – becoming the fourth youngest player to represent the club in a competitive fixture.

Despite a gallant showing against a vastly more experienced Villa side, the rookie Reds lost 5-0 but bowed out with their heads held high.

For the big FA Cup third round clash with Everton the following month, fewer changes were anticipated, but Klopp still sprung a surprise with a starting line-up that again included Williams, Jones, Elliott and Pedro Chirivella, plus debutant Nat Phillips.

Against a full-strength Blues eleven, not many gave Liverpool a chance – especially when captain James Milner was forced off through injury after just nine minutes and replaced by yet another new face in Yasser Larouci. The young Reds rose to the occasion, though, and a spectacular curling finish by Jones was good enough to seal a deserved win.

Jones was on the scoresheet again in the next round away to Shrewsbury – a game in which Williams, Larouci, Elliott and Chirivella were all given another run-out. Unfortunately, the hosts hit back to force a draw and with the replay coinciding with the first team squad's planned winter break the history books were to be rewritten for the second time in a matter of months.

Ten nights later, and with Neil Critchley back at the helm, the team that ran out in front of over 52,000 at

ARE ALRIGHT

KLOPP'S KIDS SHOW PROMISE OF A BRIGHT RED FUTURE

Anfield, was even younger than the one that played at Villa. Jones, at 19 years and 5 days old, became Liverpool's youngest ever captain and another five youngsters would be handed their senior debuts (see below). Again, the odds were stacked heavily against them, but they prevailed once more, running out 1-0 winners.

Liverpool's FA Cup run was eventually brought to a close at Chelsea in the next round but while that was quickly forgotten, the memories of seeing so many Academy graduates come of age during both domestic cup competitions in 2019/20 will linger for a long time yet.

Klopp's kids have proved to be more than alright. Hopefully there's a bright red future ahead for them.

ASTON VILLA v LIVERPOOL
Carabao Cup Quarter-Final

Avg. Age **19.5**

62 Caoimhín **Kelleher**

51 Ki-Jana **Hoever**
72 Sepp **Van den Berg**
77 Morgan **Boyes**
54 Tony **Gallacher**

55 Herbie **Kane**
68 (c) Pedro **Chirivella**
57 Isaac **Christie-Davies**

67 Harvey **Elliott**
99 Tom **Hill**
75 Luis **Longstaff**

Substitutes:
Ben **Winterbottom**, Tom **Clayton**, James **Norris***,
Elijah **Dixon-Bonner**, Leighton **Clarkson***, Jack **Bearne***,
Layton **Stewart** (*came on)

LIVERPOOL v SHREWSBURY TOWN
FA Cup 3rd Round Replay

Avg. Age **19.28**

62 Caoimhín **Kelleher**

76 Neco **Williams**
51 Ki-Jana **Hoever**
72 Sepp **Van den Berg**
46 Adam **Lewis**

84 Leighton **Clarkson**
68 Pedro **Chirivella**
80 Jake **Cain**

67 Harvey **Elliott**
49 Liam **Millar**
48 (c) Curtis **Jones**

Substitutes:
Vitezslav **Jaros**, Tony **Gallacher**, Morgan **Boyes***,
James **Norris**, Elijah **Dixon-Bonner***, Joe **Hardy***,
Jack **Bearne** (*came on)

NAME THAT TU♪♫E

Can you help fill in the blanks and work out what
popular Liverpool songs the following lyrics are taken from?

1

Let me tell you the story of a [____] boy

Who was sent far away from his home

To fight for his [____] and his country

And also the old [____] back home

SONG TITLE [____]

2

We've conquered all of [____]

We're never gonna [____]

From [____] down to Turkey

SONG TITLE [____]

3

There's something that the [____] want you to know

The best in the world his name is Bobby Firmino

Our number [____]

Give him the ball and he'll [____] every time

SONG TITLE [____]

4

We've won the English League about a

[____] times

UEFA was a simple do

We gave some exhibitions in the [____]

We are the Wembley [____] too

SONG TITLE [____]

5

At the end of a [____]

There's a [____] sky

And the sweet silver song of a [____]

SONG TITLE [____]

6

[____] is our hero, he showed us how to play

The mighty reds of [____] are out to win today

He made a team of [____], with every man a king

And every game we love to win and this is what we sin

SONG TITLE [____]

7

He's our centre half

He's our number [____]

Watch him defend

And we watch him [____]

He can pass the ball

[____] as you like

SONG TITLE [____]

8

Where once we watched the King [____]

play (and he could play)

We had Heighway on the [____]

We had [____] and songs to sing

SONG TITLE [____]

KOP QUIZ

How much can you remember about the season in which the reigning European champions conquered the world, won their first domestic league title for 30 years and also added another UEFA Super Cup to their ever-growing roll of honour?

1. Which other English club did 2019 summer signing Adrián used to play for?

2. Who scored Liverpool's goal in the Community Shield at Wembley?

3. By what score did Liverpool lead at half-time in their opening Premier League game of the season?

4. In which city did Liverpool meet Chelsea in the UEFA Super Cup final?

5. Which former Red scored against Liverpool in the second league game of the season?

6. What was the score after 90 minutes of Liverpool's Carabao Cup tie at home to Arsenal?

7. In which country did Liverpool secure qualification from the Champions League group phase?

8. Who captained Liverpool in the Carabao Cup defeat against Aston Villa?

9. Which country were Liverpool's first opponents in the 2019 FIFA Club World Cup from?

10. Name the player who scored Liverpool's last goal of 2019?

11. From which club did Liverpool sign Takumi Minamino?

12. Who provided the assist for Mo Salah's goal in the 2-0 home win over Manchester United?

13. At which ground did Liverpool's interest in the 2020 FA Cup end?

14. Who were Liverpool's first opponents when football restarted in June?

15. Liverpool clinched the Premier League title with how many games to spare?

16. Which Liverpool legend was involved in the Premier League trophy presentation?

17. How many points did Liverpool finish on in the Premier League?

18. Who was the only Liverpool player to receive a red card in 2019/20?

19. Excluding shoot-outs, how many penalties did Liverpool score in 2019/20?

20. Through the Premier League campaign, how many players did Jürgen Klopp call upon?

ANSWERS ARE ON PAGE 61

TOP OF THE WORLD

It was back in the 1960s that Bill Shankly famously spoke of his vision to build Liverpool Football Club into a 'bastion of invincibility' that would one day 'conquer the bloody world'.

Yet despite the capture of numerous domestic and European titles in the years that followed, it was not

home the FIFA Club World Cup and, in the process, clinch an unprecedented international treble.

As the reigning champions of Europe, Liverpool's participation in the tournament, along with that of their South American counterparts, began at the semi-final stage with a tie against Monterrey of Mexico.

> "WE COULDN'T DO MORE THAN WINNING THIS GAME; WINNING IT THE FIRST TIME FOR THIS WONDERFUL CLUB, THE CLUB WORLD CUP. I SAID BEFORE THE GAME I DON'T KNOW EXACTLY HOW IT WOULD FEEL. NOW I CAN SAY IT'S OUTSTANDING, ABSOLUTELY SENSATIONAL. I'M SO PROUD OF THE BOYS AND IT COULDN'T BE BETTER."
>
> Jürgen Klopp

until December 2019 that English football's most successful club was able to add global supremacy to their long list of achievements.

After failed attempts to land the coveted trophy under the competition's previous guises in 1981, 1984 and 2005, the Reds were finally able to call themselves champions of the world.

It completed a remarkable six months for Jürgen Klopp's team who, with the Champions League and UEFA Super Cup already in the bag, travelled to Doha, Qatar the week before Christmas, seeking to bring

Although Naby Keïta opened the scoring in the 12th minute, the Mexicans hit back immediately and the game drifted towards extra-time until the late intervention of substitute Robert Firmino. Sent on as an 85th minute replacement for Divock Origi, Firmino snatched victory with a winning goal in injury time.

It set up a dream final against Flamengo and gave Liverpool the chance to avenge the crushing 3-0

Liverpool's Previous World Club Finals
1981 – lost 3-0 to Flamengo
1984 – lost 1-0 to Independiente
2005 – lost 1-0 to Sao Paolo

FIFA CLUB WORLD CUP QATAR 2019™
PRESENTED BY
Alibaba Cloud

defeat they suffered at the hands of the Brazilians in Tokyo when the two clubs met to decide the 1981 World Club Championship.

A much tighter game was expected this time around and so it transpired. On a tense evening at the Khalifa National Stadium, both sides had chances but there was nothing to separate them inside 90 minutes.

As the players tired in extra-time, the prospect of a penalty shoot-out loomed, until the 99th minute when Firmino emerged the hero once again. Receiving a pass from Sadio Mané he cleverly side-stepped both a defender and the keeper before calmly rolling the ball into the net for what proved to be the winning goal.

As Jordan Henderson lifted the third trophy of the calendar year, history was made and for the first time ever, Liverpool Football Club was officially the best in the world.

The late, great Bill Shankly would have been so proud.

> "I'M DELIGHTED THAT WE'VE COME HERE AND DONE WHAT WE WANTED TO DO; AND THAT'S WIN. WE'VE HAD TWO TOUGH GAMES WITH EXTRA-TIME BUT I THOUGHT THE LADS KEPT GOING AND SHOWED A GREAT MENTALITY AGAIN TO FIND THE WINNER."

Jordan Henderson

2019 FIFA Club World Cup

1ST ROUND

Al Sadd Sports Club	3-1	Hienghene Sport

2ND ROUND

Al Hilal FC	1-0	Esperance S. de Tunis
CF Monterrey	3-2	Al Sadd Sports Club

SEMI FINAL

CR Flamengo	3-1	Al Hilal FC
CF Monterrey	1-2	LIVERPOOL

FINAL

CR Flamengo	0-1	LIVERPOOL

MY LIVERPOOL...

FABINHO TAVARES 3

"Liverpool is very important to me. When I decided to leave Monaco, I wanted to go to an important football club, that fought for huge goals, and here at Liverpool I managed to do all these things. I've also arrived at a football club where the atmosphere and the squad are great. I've learnt a lot from the technical staff as well. I've really managed to learn more at this club and understand the supporter's love closely. So I am very grateful for all these experiences I've had living here and I hope to achieve more."

JOE GOMEZ 12

"I came when I was 18, I didn't really know anything other than a little bubble in south east London. I didn't ever imagine how big the club could be and what impact it could have on my life. I could definitely say it's been the best five years of my life. I've had some tough times obviously but they have helped shape me and I wouldn't have wanted to spend them, good or bad, anywhere else. Just because of the city, the people and the club; the staff and everything that makes the club; the supporters. I've grown up here. My little boy is a Scouser now and it's home for me and there's nowhere else I'd rather be."

VIRGIL VAN DIJK

4

"I think it's very rare that you see a group of players that can actually get on with everyone. It's very special and, not only the group of players, the whole mentality of Melwood and everyone who is involved from the kitchen to the kitmen - everyone is a part of it. It's all down to the manager, everyone is involved, and I think that's a very special environment to be in. It's down to the work we do on the pitch, at the end of the day, because you need to get results. But if everyone around us is on the same page, it makes it a lot easier to go to the direction we all want to go. We all know that we have - at the moment - an unbelievable squad, a fantastic team, amazing players, maybe the best manager in the world and it's just incredible to be part of it."

ALISSON BECKER

1

"At this moment it means everything. The biggest part of my achievements in football I achieved for this club, through this club, individual and my teammates, so it means a lot to me and my family. Since we arrived here we could feel that it's a different club, a club who treats you as a family and can give you all the support that you need to play football, to stay focused on playing football. So, we are comfortable here. We love being here. We also love the warmth that we receive from the supporters, they are part of this family as well."

JORDAN **14**
HENDERSON

"What we have achieved as a team has been unbelievable and to top it off with the Premier League was really special for the lads, but also for the fans and the club. To lift that trophy is something that we've waited for, for a long time. I feel as though Liverpool has been a part of my life for so long. My kids were born here, so it's always going to be a big part of my life. It is nice to win trophies and be a part of it, hopefully there's more to come in the future. It's such a special club, a unique club and I'm so lucky, honoured and humbled to have been a part of it for so long. I hope there's many more years where I can be a part of this amazing football club and help bring success."

ALEX **15**
OXLADE-
CHAMBERLAIN

"From being a fairly inexperienced team at winning things to where we are now, this team has taken massive steps forward. You couldn't have asked for it to have gone any better for us as a group, over the last three years. Moving from one club to another you hope that these things are possible but obviously a lot of the time it doesn't always pan out as well as it has done. So, it's a credit to the team, the manager and the club in general what we've achieved so far but hopefully this is just the start of something special that we can all create together."

TRENT 66
ALEXANDER-ARNOLD

"It has been a very special few years for me, a lot of things have happened and it has all happened so fast. You don't really have time to sit back and realise what has actually happened. You just get caught up in it all. You never have time to chill and soak it all in. But I've played a lot of games, been part of such a special team and won trophies. So far, so good. It has been a good start. Winning the league was a proud moment for the club. We're really proud as a team and I'm proud to be able to see everyone in the city so happy - well, all the Liverpool fans obviously."

MOHAMED 11
SALAH

"Since I came here I said I wanted to win the Premier League with this club. What I'm seeing from the fans and the people here is unbelievable, I'm really happy and enjoying it. Always when people asked me what you prefer, Premier League or Champions League? I always say both – thankfully we've got both. That's great. It's great to win the Champions League – wow, what an achievement for the team that was. Losing the Premier League that season by one point was kind of disappointing, but we were also proud of ourselves because of how many points we got and how we played. The good thing is that we then fought back and we won it."

THE MELWOOD SCRAPBOOK

Situated four miles from Anfield, in the West Derby area of the city, is Melwood; Liverpool's training ground for the past seven decades.

Soon, the gates here will close for a final time and the entire first team operation will move to a newly built complex alongside the Academy in Kirkby.

Over the years Melwood has been such an integral part of the Liverpool story. It's been home to some of football's finest managerial, coaching and playing talent, and much of the club's success has been plotted within its boundaries.

Saying goodbye will be hard but the memories will never fade…

The original pavillion, sometime in the early to mid-50s

Heading practice for the great Billy Liddell in the 1950s

Bill Shankly puts his players through their paces in the early 1960s

Players and young supporters listening to what the manager has to say ahead of the 1963/64 title winning season

Roles reversed – Goalkeeper Tommy Lawrence attempts to score against his outfield team-mates

A warm welcome for new signing Terry McDermott from captain Emlyn Hughes and manager Bob Paisley

Bruce Grobbelaar pretending to be Superman

8 July 1984: Manager Joe Fagan observes training

Coach Ronnie Moran oversees training

New boss Roy Evans gets the players together before training in January 1994

A birds-eye view of how Melwood looked circa 1990

Sammy Lee leads from the front during pre-season training in the late 1990s

A young Jamie Carragher taking in the advice of youth coach Hughie MacAuley

It was during Gerard Houllier's reign as manager in the early 2000s that Melwood was transformed into the modern facility we know today

Talking tactics with Rafa Benitez in September 2005

These young fans clamber for the best vantage point to see their heroes train

Dirk Kuyt and Alberto Aquilani enjoying a snowball fight!

Merry Christmas 2016, festive greetings from Jürgen Klopp and his squad

Happy birthday to the boss. Jürgen Klopp celebrates turining 50 at his office in Melwood

A present day aerial shot of Melwood

IN A TWN WHERE I WAS BORN

UNITED KINGDOM

Trent Alexander-Arnold
Liverpool, England

Curtis Jones
Liverpool, England

Jordan Henderson
Sunderland, England

James Milner
Horsforth, England

Alex Oxlade-Chamberlain
Portsmouth, England

Joe Gomez
Catford, England

Harvey Elliot
Chertsey, England

Andy Robertson
Glasgow, Scotland

Neco Williams
Wrexham, Wales

SOUTH AMERICA

Alisson Becker
Novo Hamburgo, Brazil

Roberto Firmino
Maceio, Brazil

Fabinho
Campinas, Brazil

They come from far and wide, born and raised thousands of miles apart but collectively they form one team...

EUROPE

 Virgil van Dijk
Breda, Holland

Georginio Wijnaldum
Rotterdam, Holland

Divock Origi
Ostend, Belgium

Joël Matip
Bochum, Germany

Xherdan Shaqiri
Gjilan, Kosovo

Adrián
Seville, Spain

Kostas Tsimikas
Thessaloniki, Greece

ASIA

 **Takumi Minamino**
Osaka, Japan

AFRICA

 Sadio Mané
Sedhiou, Senegal

Mohamed Salah
Basyoun, Egypt

Naby Keïta
Conakry, Guinea

SADIO
SAYS

How do you always keep happy?

I'm always happy to be honest. I have plenty of reasons in life to be happy. Sometimes I can be frustrated, which is totally normal. That's part of life. But, yeah, I think I am a lucky boy.

What is your favourite thing to do on a day off?

I am going to be honest with you. I am a lazy, lazy guy. On my days off my friends always complain because I want to stay at home. I want to chill on my sofa and watch TV.

What three words would your team-mates use to describe you?

Happy. Funny. Confident.

As one of the most famous people in the world, how hard is it not to get noticed when you leave the house?

It's really not easy. I wear my cap [and pull the peak down]. Sometimes I put on a big jacket [with the hood up]. But people still notice me!

You go to mosque, what is it like?

I love going there. I am Muslim so for me, when I go there, it is really important.

There are 39 languages in Senegal, one of which is French. How do you say 'We've conquered all of Europe'?

Nous avons conquis toute l'Europe.

Can you speak some Scouse?

Come on lad. Proper Scouse now.

Is it true that you mum has never seen you play?

In my life, never. Why? I don't know. I remember at Southampton, I arranged for her to come to the stadium for the first time ever but after finishing my warm-up my uncle told me that my mum cannot watch the game, she wants to go back home.

How often do you see your family?

I see them every two or three months when I go back [to Senegal] to play with the national team.

The answers to the following questions can only be your fellow strikers Bobby and Mo…

Whose hairstyle would you swap for the day?

Sorry Mo but I think Bobby.

Who is the best dresser?

Bobby, [definitely] Bobby. Mo is sometimes terrible!

Who would win in an arm wrestle?

I would say Mo.

Who is the funniest?

Bobby.

If you had to listen to Mo or Bobby's music for a day, who would you pick?

Mo plays some music that I like. Bobby also. He plays reggaeton and I like reggaeton. So, for me, some of Bobby's and some of Mo's.

1901   1906   192

1923   1947   196

TITLE-WINNING RETRO REDS

Liverpool Football Club are champions of England for a 19th time and in clinching the club's first title for 30 years, Jürgen Klopp's team follow in the footsteps of some illustrious predecessors.

Here is a reminder of Liverpool's previous 18 title-winning teams…

196

1973   197

1977

1979

1980

1982

1983

1984

1986

1988

1990

COLOURING TIME

PREMIER LEAGUE CHAMPIONS! 2019/20

YNWA

L.F.C.

ANFIELD'S THREE GRACES

Bill Shankly, John Houlding and now Bob Paisley…take a walk around Anfield on any given day and immerse yourself in the historic splendour of three stunning sculptures.

The latest addition to an ever-expanding heritage trail around Liverpool's home ground is this eight-foot-tall bronze statue of English football's most successful manager.

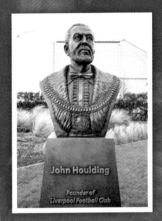

John Houlding

Founder of
Liverpool Football Club

Unveiled in January 2020, it perfectly complements the neighbouring sculptures of club founder John Houlding (opposite the Main Stand) and the legendary Bill Shankly (outside the Kop); giving those with an interest in the illustrious history of Liverpool Football Club even more of a reason to visit Anfield.

Sited outside the club store on Paisley Square, it is both a fitting tribute to the lasting legacy of an unassuming hero and deserved recognition of the outstanding contribution he made during almost half a century with the club.

During this time Paisley fulfilled a variety of roles, most notably that of manager from 1974 to 1983 - a spell in which he led the Reds to 19 trophies, including six league titles and three European Cups.

Club officials and the Paisley family worked closely with well-known local sculptor Andy Edwards to create the statue, with the iconic image used to immortalise Paisley being one of him carrying an injured Emlyn Hughes off the pitch during a match at home to Tottenham in April 1968.

A SEASON IN QUOTES

2019/20

August 13

"Tiredness, I think, is here [pointing to his head] – for sure."

Sadio Mané

August 14

"Welcome to Liverpool! It was a crazy week but with [my teammates] it's so easy playing at the back."

The recently-arrived Adrián after being the hero in the UEFA Super Cup penalty shootout victory against Chelsea

September 23

"I have to say, and it's easy to say, really thank you to the team because, how we all know, no manager can do miracles and I didn't do miracles. I just relied on a fantastic team."

Jürgen Klopp after being named Best FIFA Men's Coach for 2019

October 29

"Our identity is intensity."

Pepijn Lijnders

November 11

"It's the hardest place in Europe."

Arsene Wenger on Anfield

July 6

"We smelled really how it feels – we played the final, we won the final, we came into the city, we saw the city and saw the people. That's something you can get addicted to, you want to have that much more often."

Jürgen Klopp on the first day of pre-season after winning the Champions League

September 14

"I was close to singing it!"

Jürgen Klopp on Roberto Firmino's song after the No.9's two assists against Newcastle United

October 2

"Our mentality is that you just keep going no matter what happens."

Virgil van Dijk

November 2

"It's almost like a sixth sense."

Adam Lallana following Liverpool's comeback at Aston Villa

December 13

"It was not too bad so far, let's try to make it even better in the future."

Jürgen Klopp's message to supporters after agreeing a contract extension

"I think this may be the only trophy the club hasn't won, so to be able to do it is huge for us, putting ourselves in the history books and making sure we're remembered as a really good Liverpool team. It's an exciting time to be a Liverpool player."

Trent Alexander-Arnold after winning the FIFA Club World Cup

"I told him that we really signed Takumi Minamino from Salzburg, the guy who played against us like crazy, who was self-confident like crazy. Just be that and everything else is fine."

Jürgen Klopp on Takumi Minamino

"I don't think it's easy to measure what he does for us as a team... he's a special player and we're lucky to have him at the club."

Joe Gomez on Virgil van Dijk

"The way we play, you need to enjoy that because if you don't enjoy that then you cannot play all the games with our intensity. We try to do our best and be happy on the pitch. In Brazil we always say that you need to enjoy the game to be happy playing football because football is happiness."

Alisson Becker

"We all went through it together... it will bring us even closer in a very close group."

Andy Robertson

"If you can't get up for a game for Liverpool Football Club then I don't think you will get up for many things. The lads love playing games, we get paid to play games, we enjoy playing together and we enjoy going out there and trying to work hard and trying to achieve things and that's what we did."

Andy Robertson

"This guy is amazing."

Paris Saint-Germain's Kylian Mbappe on Trent Alexander-Arnold

"Everybody is enjoying their football but it's also about the work ethic and giving everything for each other – and that's the most important thing to me. Just give everything you can for your teammates, which we have been doing. If you do that then you get your rewards at the end."

Jordan Henderson

"Of course, we don't want to play in front of an empty stadium and we don't want games or competitions suspended, but if doing so helps one individual stay healthy - just one - we do it no questions asked."

Jürgen Klopp on the suspension of the Premier League due to the COVID-19 pandemic

"My message is: it is for you out there. It is really for you."

Jürgen Klopp to Liverpool fans after being confirmed as champions

CROSSWORD

Can you tackle this tough looking,
Kop-inspired crossword?

ACROSS

1 They won the Premier League at Anfield in 1995. (8,6)

4 The country from where Liverpool's first opponents in the 2019 FIFA Club World Cup come from. (6)

6 Number of European trophies (including Super Cup) Liverpool have won. (6)

9 The area of Anfield between the Kop and the Kenny Dalglish stand is more commonly known as _____ corner. (8)

12 The number of times Liverpool have won the FA Cup. (5)

13 Nickname of the club from whom Liverpool signed Jordan Henderson. (3,5,4)

14 _____ Jones, scorer of Liverpool's winning goal in the 2020 FA Cup 3rd round against Everton. (6)

DOWN

2 He captained Liverpool to victory when they last won a trophy at Wembley. (6,7)

3 Virgil Van Dijk's first British club. (6)

5 The new statue at Anfield features which former Liverpool captain on Bob Paisley's back. (5,6)

7 The only Liverpool manager with an unbeaten record in European competition. (3,7)

8 Liverpool's opponents on the opening weekend of the 2019/20 Premier League season. (7,4)

10 The city where Liverpool won the 2005 Champions League and 2019 UEFA Super Cup. (8)

11 Jürgen Klopp's middle name. (7)

ANSWERS ARE ON PAGE 61

ROBBO AND MILLY'S GOAT List

Andy Robertson and James Milner have not only developed a great understanding on the pitch for Liverpool, they've also established themselves as the go-to double-act for LFCTV's digital producers.

The pair have starred in a number of hilarious videos that have received widespread acclaim across the club's online and social media channels.

One particular strand of content they have made their own has been the GOAT (Greatest Of All-Time) List series in which they are tasked with tackling an age-old debate by whittling down a shortlist then coming up with their personal favourites.

Here's the outcome of their first three episodes...

British Sitcoms

Photo credit: PA Images

1. Only Fools And Horses
2. The Inbetweeners
3. Gavin & Stacey
4. Fawlty Towers
5. The Office

Dunking Biscuits

1. Custard Creams
2. Jammie Dodgers
3. Chocolate Digestives
4. Ginger Nuts
5. Shortbread

Christmas Films

Photo credit: Shooting Star/SIPA USA

1. Home Alone
2. Elf
3. Home Alone 2
4. Love Actually
5. Die Hard

IT'S A FACT

2019/20: LFC'S UNFORGETTABLE SEASON

Compiled by club statistician Ged Rea

24 Liverpool achieved the longest run of successive home league victories (24), breaking their own English record of 21.

They reached 30 league wins faster than any team in English top-flight history, in just 34 games (beating Manchester City's 35 matches).

79 POINTS OUT OF 81

Jürgen Klopp's men recorded the best ever start to a season by any team in Europe's top five leagues – 26 wins and a draw from their first 27 games – taking 79 points out of 81 on offer.

104 POINTS

During the course of a 38-game spell across two seasons, the Reds accrued more points than any other team in Premier League history – 104.

Liverpool clinched the Premier League title in just 31 games and broke the English top-flight record by winning it with seven fixtures to spare, bettering the five set by Manchester United (twice), Everton and Manchester City.

They equalled the Premier League record for most points accumulated at home in a season – 55 – with 18 wins and one draw. Chelsea (2005-06), Manchester United (2010-11) and Manchester City (2011-12) are the others to have set the landmark.

FOR THE FIRST TIME IN THEIR HISTORY, LIVERPOOL BEAT EVERY TEAM IN A LEAGUE SEASON.

32 LEAGUE WINS

The Reds equalled an English football record for the top two divisions of 32 league wins in a season, set by Manchester City in 2017-18 and 2018-19, and Tottenham Hotspur in Division 2 in 1919-20.

By recording those 32 wins they also set a club record, beating the 30 won in 1978-79 (42 games) and last season (38 games).

4

The Reds won a British-record fourth European Super Cup.

27 DAYS

They also became the first team in English top-flight history to play in five different competitions within the space of 27 days.

THEY EQUALLED THE PREMIER LEAGUE RECORD OF 18 CONSECUTIVE LEAGUE VICTORIES, WHICH ALSO SET A NEW CLUB RECORD.

1

Klopp's side occupied top spot in the league for each of the last 37 rounds and were only off the summit for seven of the 352 days the campaign lasted. They led every day since August 17.

99 POINTS

They set a new club record of 99 points in a season – one more than the 98 gained in a 42-game season in 1978-79 (adjusted to three points for a win).

Liverpool remained unbeaten at Anfield for a third consecutive league season for the first time in their history.

THEY ARE NOW THE FIRST TEAM IN HISTORY TO WIN THE LEAGUE TITLE IN AN EIGHTH DIFFERENT DECADE, BEATING ARSENAL, EVERTON AND MANCHESTER UNITED'S SEVEN.

8 WINS

By winning their opening eight league games of this season they became the first team ever in top-flight history to achieve the feat twice.

13 LEAGUE 'DOUBLES'

They set a new club record of 13 league 'doubles' in a season, bettering last season (12) and in doing so also equalled the English top-flight record.

Becoming the first British team ever to hold the European Cup, European Super Cup, FIFA Club World Cup and league titles simultaneously.

ALL-TIME APPEARANCES

1.	Ian Callaghan	857
2.	Jamie Carragher	737
3.	Steven Gerrard	710
4.	Ray Clemence, Emlyn Hughes	665
5.	Ian Rush	660
6.	Phil Neal	650
7.	Tommy Smith	638
8.	Bruce Grobbelaar	628
9.	Alan Hansen	620
10.	Chris Lawler	549

CONSECUTIVE APPEARANCES

1.	Phil Neal	417
2.	Ray Clemence	336
3.	Bruce Grobbelaar	317
4.	Chris Lawler	316
5.	David James	212
6.	Alan Kennedy	205
7.	Ian Callaghan	185
8.	Kenny Dalglish	180
9.	Emlyn Hughes	177
10.	Peter Thompson	153

GAMES AS CAPTAIN

1.	Steven Gerrard	473
2.	Ron Yeats	416
3.	Emlyn Hughes	337
4.	Alex Raisbeck	267
5.	Donald Mackinlay	265
6.	Sami Hyypia	204
7.	Alan Hansen	195
8.	Jordan Henderson	171
9.	Tommy Smith	158
10.	Phil Thompson & Graeme Souness	147

GOALSCORERS (all competitions)

1.	Ian Rush	346
2.	Roger Hunt	285
3.	Gordon Hodgson	241
4.	Billy Liddell	228
5.	Steven Gerrard	186
6.	Robbie Fowler	183
7.	Kenny Dalglish	172
8.	Michael Owen	158
9.	Harry Chambers	151
10.	Sam Raybould	130

Most Medals Won (not including Charity/Community Shield)

1.	Phil Neal	18
2.	Alan Hansen	17
3.	Kenny Dalglish, Phil Thompson	15
4.	Ian Rush	14
5.	Ian Callaghan, Ray Clemence, Bruce Grobbelaar	13
6.	Steve Heighway, Graeme Souness, Ronnie Whelan	12
7.	Alan Kennedy, Ray Kennedy, Terry McDermott	11
8.	Jimmy Case, Emlyn Hughes, Mark Lawrenson, Sammy Lee, Tommy Smith	10
9.	Jamie Carragher, David Fairclough, Craig Johnston	9
10.	Steven Gerrard, David Johnson, Steve Nicol	8

GOALKEEPER CLEAN SHEETS

1.	Ray Clemence	323
2.	Bruce Grobbelaar	268
3.	Pepe Reina	177
4.	Elisha Scott	137
5.	Tommy Lawrence	133
6.	David James	103
7.	Jerzy Dudek	77
8.	Arthur Riley	69
9.	Simon Mignolet	66
10.	Sam Hardy	63

PENALTY SCORERS

1.	Steven Gerrard	47
2.	Jan Molby	42
3.	Phil Neal	38
4.	Billy Liddell	34
5.	Tommy Smith	22
6.	Robbie Fowler	20
7.	James Milner	19
8.	John Aldridge	17
9.	Terry McDermott, Gordon Hodgson	16
10.	Michael Owen	13

Our leading goal scorer (346), Ian Rush

Ian Callaghan, 1st in all time appearances (857)

Steve Gerrard, 473 games as captain!

PENALTY SAVES

1.	**Sam Hardy**	**10**
2.	Elisha Scott	9
3.	Bruce Grobbelaar, Simon Mignolet	8
4.	Ray Clemence	7
5.	Arthur Riley, Cyril Sidlow	6
6.	David James	5
7.	Kenneth Campbell, Pepe Reina	4
8.	Ned Doig, Tommy Lawrence	3
9.	Harry Storer, Peter Platt, Augustus Beeby, Ray Minshull, Jerzy Dudek	2
10.	Charles Cotton, Dirk Kemp, Charlie Ashcroft, Dave Underwood, Mike Hooper, Sander Westerveld, Chris Kirkland, Brad Jones, Loris Karius	1

Ray Clemence

ANFIELD ATTENDANCES

1.	**v Wolverhampton Wanderers, FA Cup 4th round, 2 February 1952**	**61,905**
2.	v Tranmere Rovers, FA Cup 4th round, 27 January 1934	61,036
3.	v Notts County, FA Cup 4th round, 29 January 1949	61,003
4.	v Chelsea, First Division, 27 December 1949	58,757
5.	v Burnley, FA Cup 4th round replay, 20 February 1963	57,905
6.	v Chelsea, FA Cup quarter-final, 27 February 1932	57,804
7.	v Middlesbrough, First Division, 23 October 1948	57,561
8.	v Bolton Wanderers, First Division, 11 September 1948	56,561
9.	v Leicester City, First Division, 28 April 1973	56,202
10.	v Burnley, First Division, 6 September 1947	56,074

BIGGEST WINS

1.	**v Stromsgodset (1974)**	**11-0**
2.	v Dundalk (1969), Fulham (1986)	10-0
3.	v Rotherham Town (1896), Oulu Palloseura (1980)	10-1
4.	v Newtown (1892), Crystal Palace (1989)	9-0
5.	v Higher Walton (1892), Burnley (1928), TSV Munich (1967), Swansea City (1990), Stoke City (2000), Besiktas (2007)	8-0
6.	v Grimsby Town (1902)	9-2
7.	v Burslem Port Vale (1905)	8-1
8.	v Fleetwood Rangers (1892), Burton Swifts (1896), Crewe Alexandra (1896), Stoke City (1902), Fulham (1955), Tottenham (1978), Oulu Palloseura (1981), York City (1985), Rochdale (1996), Birmingham City (2006), NK Maribor (2017), Spartak Moscow (2017)	7-0
9.	v Portsmouth (1927)	8-2
10.	v Newton Heath (1895), Grimsby Town (1936), Derby County (1991), Southampton (1999)	7-1

LIVERPOOL FC
2020/21

4

VIRGIL
VAN DIJK

12

JOE
GOMEZ

21

KOSTAS
TSIMIKAS

26

ANDY
ROBERTSON

76

NECO
WILLIAMS

3

FABINHO

5

GEORGINIO
WIJNALDUM

7

JAMES
MILNER

23

XHERDAN
SHAQIRI

67

HARVEY
ELLIOTT

9

ROBERTO
FIRMINO

10

SADIO
MANÉ

JÜRGEN KLOPP

ALISSON BECKER

ADRIÁN

CAOIMHÍN KELLEHER

JOËL MATIP

KI-JANA HOEVER

TRENT ALEXANDER-ARNOLD

SEPP VAN DEN BERG

NABY KEÏTA

JORDAN HENDERSON

ALEX OXLADE-CHAMBERLAIN

CURTIS JONES

MOHAMED SALAH

TAKUMI MINAMINO

DIVOCK ORIGI

57

The Cham

League
Titles

European Cup/
UEFA Champions
League

FA Cups

19

6

7

CHA

pions Wall

A Cups

League Cups

UEFA
Super Cups

FIFA Club
World Cup

3

8

4

1

COMPETITION!

TO WIN A SIGNED 2020/21 SHIRT ANSWER THE FOLLOWING QUESTION...

 How many times has Liverpool Football Club been champions of England?

A: 19
B: 18
C: 17

Entry is by email only. Only one entry per contestant. Please enter LFC SHIRT followed by either A, B or C in the subject line of an email. In the body of the email, please include your full name, address, postcode, email address and phone number and send to - frontdesk@grangecommunications.co.uk by Friday 31st March 2021.

Terms & Conditions

1. The closing date for this competition is Tuesday 31st March 2021 at midnight. Entries received after that time will not be counted.
2. Information on how to enter and on the prizes form part of these conditions.
3. Entry is open to those residing in the UK only. If entrants are under 18, consent from a parent or guardian must be obtained and the parent or guardian must agree to these terms and conditions.
4. This competition is not open to employees or their relatives of Liverpool FC. Any such entries will be invalid.
5. The start date for entries is 31st October 2020 at 4pm.
6. Entries must be strictly in accordance with these terms and conditions. Any entry not in strict accordance with these terms and conditions will be deemed to be invalid and no prizes will be awarded in respect of such entry. By entering, all entrants will be deemed to accept these rules.
7. One (1) lucky winner will win a 2020/2021 season signed football shirt.
8. The prize is non-transferable and no cash alternative will be offered. Entry is by email only. Only one entry per contestant. Please enter LFC SHIRT followed by either A, B or C in the subject line of an email. In the body of the email, please include your full name, address, postcode, email address and phone number and send to: frontdesk@grangecommunications.co.uk by Tuesday 31st March 2021.
9. The winner will be picked at random. The winner will be contacted within 72 hours of the closing date. Details of the winners can be requested after this time from the address below.
10. Entries must not be sent in through agents or third parties. No responsibility can be accepted for lost, delayed, incomplete, or for electronic entries or winning notifications that are not received or delivered. Any such entries will be deemed void.
11. The winners shall have 72 hours to claim their prize once initial contact has been made by the Promoter. Failure to respond may result in forfeiture of the prize.
12. The Promoter reserves the right to withdraw or amend the promotion as necessary due to circumstances outside its reasonable control. The Promoter's decision on all matters is final and no correspondence will be entered into.
13. The Promoter (or any third party nominated by the Promoter) may use the winner's name and image and their comments relating to the prize for future promotional, marketing and publicity purposes in any media worldwide without notice or without any fee being paid.
14. Liverpool Football Club's decision is final; no correspondence will be entered into. Except in respect of death or personal injury resulting from any negligence of the Club, neither The Liverpool Football Club nor any of its officers, employees or agents shall be responsible for (whether in tort, contract or otherwise):
    - (i) any loss, damage or injury to you and/or any guest or to any property belonging to you or any guest in connection with this competition and/or the prize, resulting from any cause whatsoever;
    - (ii) for any loss of profit, loss of use, loss of opportunity or any indirect, economic or consequential losses whatsoever;
15. This competition shall be governed by English law.
16. Promoter: Grange Communications, 22 Great King Street, Edinburgh EH3 6QH

THE ANSWERS!

WORDSEARCH

```
W M  D E T I N U D L E I F F E H S  K B
X  Y  K W T M P Z F M M  H  C K Q  H  M R F
L  K  T N L R P G R A  P  C V G M  T  E Y D
F  L  N I C R V N L F T  I  N N R U  M  E T E
B  K  N G C J J L Y M  K  W G X B O  E  D T I
B  U  M G N R I  B  A Q T R L P L M  R  T N N
V  M  R T R V E H R N N O T K T E  T  O U R
L  H  J N N E T T V I M N L M N N  O  N R E
Q  K  K O L S T T S H G N V Y H R  N  E S T
H  L  T N E E V S F E O H K P K U  M  A E H
L  S  Q W N K Y T E T H C T W O B  A  H N A
A  P  N K T M M P C H C A O V  B  L  N N L N
A  R  S E N A L M W E I T N H N L  M  E C A
J  K  N Y C R A B L B F E K A R T  F  F C E
J  T  K G R H M S N O M T L R M  F  E C C A
K  W  C T T L E Z R P G K N L C N  T  F N A
K  X  K U V A T D S E V L O W  M  J T B A M
M  H  O M B W V L Q F F R G N N N  O  T B M T
M  S  C R Y S T A L P A L A C E G  T  N Q
```

CROSSWORD

```
B L A C K B U R N R O V E R S        C
                          T          E
      M E X I C O   T W E L V E       L
      M             N     V          T
R     M             O     E          I
O   F L A G P O L E  R     N          C
Y   I               W     G
H   S               I     E
O   T               C     R
D   A               H     R
G   N               C     A
S E V E N     T H E B L A C K C A T S
O   B               T     D
N   C U R T I S     Y
    U
    L
```

NAME THAT TUNE

1 Let me tell you the story of a poor boy
   Who was sent far away from his home
   To fight for his king and his country
   And also the old folks back home
   Song title: Poor Scouser Tommy

2 We've conquered all of Europe
   We're never gonna stop
   From Paris down to Turkey
   Song title: Allez Allez Allez

3 There's something that the Kop want
   you to know
   The best in the world his name is Bobby Firmino
   Our number nine
   Give him the ball and he'll score every time
   Song title: Si Senor

4 We've won the English League about a
   thousand times
   UEFA was a simple do
   We gave some exhibitions in the FA Cup
   We are the Wembley wizards too
   Song title: Every Other Saturday

5 At the end of a storm
   There's a golden sky
   And the sweet silver song of a lark
   Song title: You'll Never Walk Alone

6 Shankly is our hero, he showed us how to play
   The mighty reds of Europe are out to win today
   He made a team of champions, with every man a king
   And every game we love to win and this is what we sing
   Song title: We Love You Liverpool

7 He's our centre half
   He's our number four
   Watch him defend
   And we watch him score
   He can pass the ball
   Calm as you like
   Song title: Virgil van Dijk

8 Where once we watched the King
   Kenny play (and he could play)
   We had Heighway on the wing
   We had dreams and songs to sing
   Song title: Fields Of Anfield Road

SEASON QUIZ

1. West Ham United
2. Joël Matip
3. 4-0
4. Istanbul
5. Danny Ings
6. 5-5
7. Austria
8. Pedro Chirivella
9. Mexico
10. Sadio Mané
11. Red Bull Salzburg
12. Alisson Becker
13. Stamford Bridge
14. Everton
15. Seven
16. Kenny Dalglish
17. 99
18. Alisson Becker
19. Six
20. 24

SPOT THE DIFFERENCE

DIFFERENCES